W9-CEV-597

ENDANGERED
ANIMALS OF
ASIA

WORLD
BOOK

a Scott Fetzer company
Chicago
worldbook.com

Staff

Executive Committee

President
Donald D. Keller
Vice President and Editor in Chief
Paul A. Kobasa
Vice President, Sales
Sean Lockwood
Vice President, Finance
Anthony Doyle
Director, Marketing
Nicholas A. Fryer
Director, Human Resources
Bev Ecker

Editorial

Associate Director,
Annuals and Topical Reference
Scott Thomas
Managing Editor,
Annuals and Topical Reference
Barbara A. Mayes
Senior Editor,
Annuals and Topical Reference
Christine Sullivan
Manager, Indexing Services
David Pofelski
Administrative Assistant
Ethel Matthews
Manager, Contracts & Compliance
(Rights & Permissions)
Loranne K. Shields

Editorial Administration

Senior Manager, Publishing
Operations
Timothy Falk

Manufacturing/ Production

Director
Carma Fazio
Manufacturing Manager
Sandra Johnson
Production/Technology
Manager
Anne Fritzinger
Proofreader
Nathalie Strassheim

Graphics and Design

Art Director
Tom Evans
Senior Designer
Don Di Sante
Media Researcher
Jeff Heimsath
Manager, Cartographic Services
Wayne K. Pichler
Senior Cartographer
John M. Rejba

Marketing

Marketing Specialists
Alannah Sharry
Annie Suhy
Digital Marketing Specialists
Iris Liu
Nudrat Zoha

Writer

A. J. Smuskiewicz

The cover image is the endangered snow leopard.

World Book, Inc.
233 North Michigan Avenue
Chicago, Illinois 60601 U.S.A.

For information about other World Book publications, visit our website at **www.worldbook.com** or call **1-800-WORLDBK (967-5325).**
For information about sales to schools and libraries, call 1-800-975-3250 (United States) or 1-800-837-5365 (Canada).

Library of Congress Cataloging-in-Publication Data

Endangered animals of Asia.
   pages cm. -- (Endangered animals of the world)
  Summary: "Information about some of the more important and interesting endangered animals of Asia, including the animal's common name, scientific name, and conservation status; also includes a map showing the range of each animal featured; and a glossary, additional resources, and an index"-- Provided by publisher
  Includes index.
  ISBN 978-0-7166-5622-7
  1. Endangered species--Asia--Juvenile literature. I. World Book, Inc.
QL737.C23E58 2015
591.68095--dc23

           2014019654

Endangered Animals of the World
ISBN: 978-0-7166-5620-3 (set)

Printed in China by Shenzhen Donnelley Printing Co., Ltd. Guangdong Province
1st printing October 2014

Contents

Why species in Asia are threatened

For thousands of years, people in China and other parts of Asia have used the body parts of wild animals to make medicines for various health problems. For example, rhinoceros horns are ground into a powder that is believed to cure illnesses from fever to cancer. Tiger bones are boiled and ground to make "tiger wine," to treat pain, ulcers, and malaria.

The medical use of wild animal parts stems from the ancient belief that such products will help restore a vital balance between the human body and the natural world. The continued demand for these body parts—not only in Asia but also in the United States and elsewhere—is a major reason why many animal *species* in Asia are endangered. (A species is a group of animals that have certain permanent characteristics in common and are able to *interbreed* [mate].) However, no scientific evidence indicates that these remedies work. In fact, some of them may cause poisoning, allergy attacks, and other serious problems. Asian animals are also hunted for food and for sale as pets. Many tortoises and turtles in Asia are killed for all three reasons.

An estimated 3,100 species in Asia are threatened, many critically. Of course, this number includes only those species known to science. Many species remain undiscovered. And almost certainly, a number of these animals are in peril or have even disappeared.

The exploding human population in much of Asia means that more and more wildlife *habitats* (living areas) are being turned into farmland, logging sites, roadways, and shopping malls. Chemical pollution from industries and farms poisons habitats. For many poor nations in Asia, such environmental problems are not nearly as important as building up their economic power. So government officials often simply ignore the environmental and wildlife problems.

Conservationists have achieved some successes in Asia. One of the greatest of these successes—returning the Przewalski's horse to the wild, where it had become extinct—is described on pages 44-45. The creation of the vast Seima Protection Forest in Cambodia in 2009 was another great success. The forest is home to many endangered species, including the largest populations of two monkeys—the black-shanked douc and the yellow-cheeked crested gibbon.

A number of other conservation efforts have picked up steam in Asia since about 2000. Those efforts have often been led by international conservation organizations that worked hard to get the cooperation of regional governments.

In this volume. The species presented in this volume represent a variety of endangered animals in Asia. From the smallest and simplest to the largest and most powerful, the continent's wildlife is facing never-ending challenges from humans, including *poachers* (illegal hunters) and those who seek to use land for their own purposes.

Scientific sequence. These species are presented in a standard scientific sequence that generally goes from simple to complex. This sequence starts with insects or other *invertebrates* (animals without backbones) and then moves through fish, amphibians, reptiles, birds, and mammals.

Range. Red areas on maps indicate an animal's *range* (area in which it lives naturally) on the Asian continent.

Glossary: Italicized words, except for scientific names, appear with their definitions in the Glossary at the end of the book.

Conservation status. Each species discussed in this book is listed with its common name, scientific name, and conservation status. The conservation status tells how seriously a species is threatened. Unless noted differently, the status is according to the International Union for Conservation of Nature (IUCN), a global organization of conservation groups. The most serious IUCN status is *Extinct,* followed by *Extinct in the Wild, Critically Endangered, Endangered, Vulnerable, Near Threatened,* and *Least Concern.* Criteria, or rules, used to determine these conservation statuses are listed to the right.

Conservation statuses

Extinct All individuals of the species have died

Extinct in the Wild The species is no longer observed in its past range

Critically Endangered The species will become extinct unless immediate conservation action is taken

Endangered The species is at high risk of becoming extinct due to a large decrease in range, population, or both

Vulnerable The species is at some risk of becoming extinct due to a moderate decrease in range, population, or both

Near Threatened The species is likely to become threatened in the future

Least Concern The species is common throughout its range

Icons. The icons indicate various threats that have made animals vulnerable to extinction.

Key to icons

 Habitat loss

 Pet trade

 Hunting

 Pollution

Poecilotheria formosa

Conservation status: Endangered

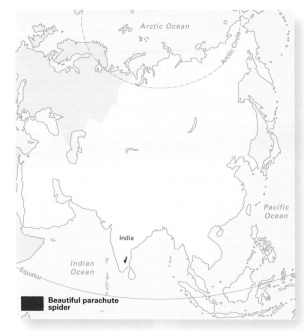

The beautiful parachute spider is a *species* (type) of tarantula that has black and tan stripes on its long, hairy legs. The name "parachute spider" refers to the method used by young spiders to disperse—that is, to spread to new areas. The small, young spider casts a thread of silk into the breeze, and winds carry the spider away as if the silk thread were a parachute or balloon.

In most cases, this technique carries the spider several feet away. However, some parachute spiders have been known to travel many miles with the wind. Most other knowledge about the behavior of beautiful parachute spiders comes from observations in captivity.

Habitat. The parachute spider lives in forests in the Eastern Ghats Mountains of southern India. These forest *habitats* (living areas) are highly disturbed because of widespread cutting of trees for firewood and timber.

Threats. Both habitat disturbance and the pet trade threaten the population of the spider. Roads and other human *developments* (activities that affect the natural environment) have broken up the spider's habitat. The spider is known from only a few isolated locations. Spiders captured from those locations are sold on the international pet market.

Conservation. Conservationists have urged the Indian government to grant the beautiful parachute spider protection under that country's Wildlife Protection Act.

The beautiful parachute spider is often sold on the international pet market.

Poecilotheria metallica

Conservation status: Critically Endangered

The body of the Gooty tarantula—also known as the peacock tarantula—is an unusual, striking shade of brilliant blue.

Habitat. This spider is known to live in only one small location—less than 39 square miles (100 square kilometers) in size—in a *deciduous forest* (with leaf-shedding trees) in the Andhra Pradesh region of southern India. These spiders live mainly inside the holes of trees. There, they make funnel-shaped webs on which they lay in wait for flying insects to capture as food. They may have a leg span of 8 inches (20 centimeters) when fully grown.

Threats. Like the forest inhabited by the beautiful parachute spider, the Gooty tarantula's forest *habitat* (living place) is highly disturbed and broken up by firewood collection and logging activities. Because of its beautiful color, this *species* (type) of tarantula is highly prized as a pet, with adults selling for more than $500! In 2012, the International Union for

Gooty tarantula

Conservation of Nature (IUCN) placed the Gooty tarantula on its list of 100 most endangered species.

The body of the Gooty tarantula is a fantastic shade of blue with yellow markings.

Hippocampus barbouri

Conservation status: Vulnerable

The colors of the Barbour's seahorse vary. Some are white or yellow, while others are greenish or brownish. Still others have reddish spots or lines on the hard plates that cover their bodies. They range in size from about 4 to 6 inches (11 to 15 centimeters), including the tail.

Habitat. Barbour's seahorse is the only seahorse *species* (type) that lives solely in the waters of Southeast Asia, with populations off the coasts of Indonesia, Malaysia, and the Philippines. They are often found clinging to seagrass and coral reefs with their *prehensile* (grasping) tails.

Reproduction. As in all seahorses, the male Barbour's seahorse has a pouch in which the female lays her eggs. The male carries the eggs inside its pouch until they hatch into tiny young.

Threats. Thousands of these beautiful, spiny seahorses have been sold for the international aquarium trade, though their declining numbers have made them difficult to find today.

The Barbour's seahorse is also killed for use in traditional Chinese medicines. They are sometimes caught accidentally through certain fishing practices, such as trawling with large nets.

Yet another threat to the Barbour's seahorse is the destruction of its shallow seagrass *habitat* (living area) by loose dirt and other matter called *silt* in the water. The silt results from soil erosion caused by forestry and agricultural activities.

The biggest threat to the Barbour's seahorse is the international pet trade. People enjoy adding these creatures to their saltwater aquariums.

Barbour's seahorse

Pangasianodon gigas

Conservation status: Critically Endangered

With some individuals growing to a length of 9.8 feet (3 meters) and a weight of 770 pounds (349 kilograms), the Thailand giant catfish is the largest freshwater fish in the world. It has a fast growth rate for a fish, adding about 440 pounds (200 kilograms) to its weight in the first six years of its life.

Habitat. This catfish lives in rivers and lakes, being most common in the Mekong River basin in Thailand. Biologists believe that the Thailand giant catfish *migrates* (moves) from the lower Mekong basin upstream into Cambodia once a year to *spawn* (lay eggs). The fish eats mostly algae and plant detritus—decayed material—that it finds on river or lake bottoms.

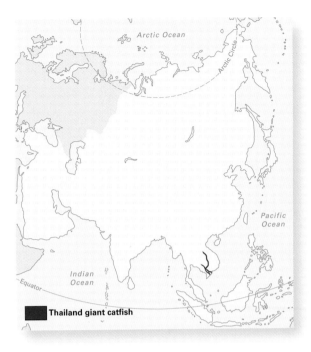

Thailand giant catfish

Threats. By the 1970's, fishermen were reporting that the giant catfish was becoming more difficult to find—the result of many decades of overfishing. Destruction of their *habitat* (living area), including the damming of rivers, is another threat. Other habitat problems have been caused by excessive soil and *silt* (tiny pieces of clay and other matter) entering the Mekong basin because of forestry practices in the area.

Conservation. To try to save the giant catfish, the Thai government has released thousands of captive-bred giant catfish into the Mekong River basin.

The Thailand giant catfish is the world's largest freshwater fish. It was once plentiful in the Mekong River Basin in Thailand.

Andrias davidianus

Conservation status: Critically Endangered

The world's largest salamander, the Chinese giant salamander has been known to grow to a length of 6 feet (1.8 meters). However, since the population of this *species* (type) began crashing in the 1980's, most individuals found in the wild are much smaller. Some biologists speculate that excessive collecting and killing of these animals may have somehow interrupted their ability to grow to grow to a large size.

Description. This amphibian has rough, wrinkled, blotchy-colored skin that may be

greenish, brown, or black. As in many other amphibians, wet skin serves as a site of gas exchange, where oxygen is taken in through tiny *pores* (holes) in the skin and carbon dioxide is released.

Diet and habitat. The Chinese giant salamander is *nocturnal* (active at night), using its senses of smell and touch to move around its river *habitat* (living area) and find food. It has tiny eyes on the top of its flat head, and its vision is poor.

This big salamander hides in spaces that it finds along riverbanks, between rocks, or under water. When it hunts, it snatches worms, insects, crayfish, crabs, snails, fish, or other amphibians with a quick bite of its large mouth. The Chinese giant salamander is most common in central and southern China, where it occurs in several small populations that are separated from each other by roads, farmland, and other human *developments* (activities that change the natural environment).

Threats. Biologists estimate that the total population of the Chinese giant salamander has declined by more than 80 percent since the 1980's. At that time, people began to kill large numbers of the salamanders for food. The meat of these animals is considered a favored delicacy in Chinese cuisine.

Other factors have also had severe impacts on their population in the wild. Forests near the rivers where they live have been destroyed. Chemical compounds from mining and farming activities have polluted their river habitats. Some of the rivers have been dammed, which changed their natural flow.

Conservation. Chinese giant salamanders are raised in zoos and a number of protected nature reserves. These reserves play an important role in preserving this species, whose natural habitat continues to disappear under the pressures of an exploding human population.

Chinese giant salamandeers are also bred and raised on commercial farms. But the farm-raised salamanders are sold for food. They are not used to build up the wild population.

Although threatened by habitat loss, the Chinese giant salamander became critically endangered largely because the meat of these animals is now considered a delicacy in Chinese cuisine.

Manouria emys

Conservation status: Endangered

The Asian giant tortoise, which is also called the Asian brown tortoise, is the largest tortoise in Asia and one of the largest in the world. It can grow to a length of 20 inches (50 centimeters) and a weight of 44 pounds (20 kilograms).

Appearance. The reptile has a *carapace* (upper shell) that is various shades of brown or black. On both sides of the tail are clusters of scales that are so large, they almost look like extra feet—giving the animal another alternate name, the "six-footed tortoise."

Subspecies and habitats. Biologists divide the Asian giant tortoise into two *subspecies* (divisions of a *species* [animal type]). The larger and darker subspecies is found in Bangladesh, India, Myanmar, and northern Thailand. The smaller and lighter subspecies is found in southern Thailand, Malaysia, Borneo, and Sumatra.

Reproduction. The Asian giant tortoise has unusually complex forms of communication and courtship. Males show their claims on nearby females by making loud calls to frighten away other males. When the male courts the female, he repeatedly bobs his head up and down and point it toward her as he walks around her. Before mounting her to mate, he walks close behind her as they call at each other.

The female lays her eggs in a nest she makes of *detritus* (decayed plant material) on the ground. She protects the eggs until they hatch, chasing away animals she sees as threats. Asian giant tortoises are known to live for a very long time—approximately 150 years.

Threats. The Asian giant is one of many species of Asian turtles and tortoises whose populations have been gutted by over-harvesting for food, traditional medicines, and the pet trade. Its large size makes it fairly easy for de-

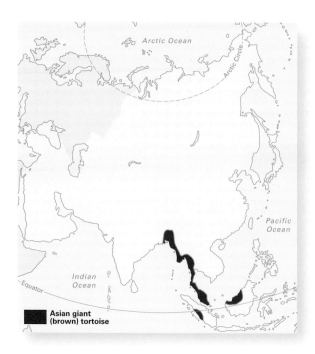

Asian giant
(brown) tortoise

termined hunters and collectors to track down. And a lot of money can be made by selling these animals on the international black, or unlawful, market.

In addition, much of the tortoise's forest *habitat* (living area) has been destroyed by human activities. As a result, the reptile can be found only in small populations that are widely separated from each other.

Conservation. Trade involving the endangered Asian giant tortoise is regulated by international treaties and various laws. For example, Malaysia sets annual quotas on the number of tortoises that can be legally exported.

The European Union has banned the import of all Asian giant tortoises. Despite such legal protections, the long-term survival of the species remains in doubt.

The very long-lived Asian giant tortoise has been over-harvested for food and traditional medicines. Although trade in the species is regulated by international treaties, the tortoises are sold on the black market for large amounts of money.

Alligator sinensis

Conservation status: Critically Endangered

At 5 feet (1.5 meters) long, the Chinese alligator is one of the smallest crocodilians (a group that includes alligators and crocodiles). By contrast, the American alligator's average length is 10 feet (3 meters). The hard, rough scales along the Chinese alligator's back and tail have a yellowish-greenish-gray color, and the reptile has black spots on its lower jaw. The *snout* (nose) of this alligator turns up at the front.

Habitat and diet. Chinese alligators live in the Yangtze River basin and associated *wetlands* along China's central Pacific Ocean coast. (Wetlands are areas where the ground remains soaked with water for most of the year.) According to historical records, these alligators used to live in additional parts of China as well as in Korea. They prey on a variety of animals, including fish, snails, clams, waterfowl, and mammals.

Chinese alligators spend most of winter inside their burrows, which they dig about 3.3 feet (1 meter) deep into the banks of wetland rivers. Upon emerging in the spring, the reptiles bask in the sun to warm up.

Reproduction. Males mate with several females in the same breeding season. The female builds a mound-shaped nest on the land from mud and vegetation. The nest is usually built near an underground burrow in which the female rests. She lays as many as 40 eggs in a depression at the top of the mound, covering them with plant material to hide and *incubate* them (keep them warm so they will hatch). She guards the nest and eggs for about 70 days, until the hatchlings break out. The mother may remain with her young through the first winter.

The sex of the developing alligators inside the eggs is controlled by the temperature of the eggs. Females develop in eggs that have an incubation temperatures below 82 °F (28 °C), and males grow in eggs at temperatures above

Chinese alligator

91 °F (33 °C). In eggs at temperatures in-between, more-or-less equal numbers of males and females will develop.

Threats. Chinese alligators have been classified as an endangered *species* (type) since the 1980's. Only a few hundred individuals are thought to survive in the wild. The main threat they face is the destruction of their wetland *habitats* (living areas) in China. The wetlands are also affected by agricultural *developments* (activities) and pollution.

These alligators are also hunted by people for their meat and their internal organs, which are used to make traditional Chinese medicines. They are not hunted for the hides on their bellies—like some alligators—because they are covered with *osteoderms* (hard bony plates). Thousands of Chinese alligators exist in captivity, offering a possible source of animals for efforts to rebuild the wild population.

The Chinese alligator is about half the size of the American alligator. Unlike its American cousin, the Chinese alligator is critically endangered.

Gavialis gangeticus

Conservation status: Critically Endangered

The gavial, also called the gharial, differs from other crocodilians by having a long, very narrow *snout* (nose). It uses its snout to capture fish and aquatic *invertebrates* (animals without backbones) underwater. The narrow snout offers little resistance to water, so it can be swished through the water quickly to catch prey. At the tip of the snout on the adult male is a bulbous structure that resembles a type of Indian pot called a "ghara."

Appearance. One of the largest crocodilians, the gavial can grow to a length of more than 20 feet (6 meters). Males are larger than females. When the young hatch from eggs that the female lays in sandbanks, they are already about 15 inches (38 centimeters) long.

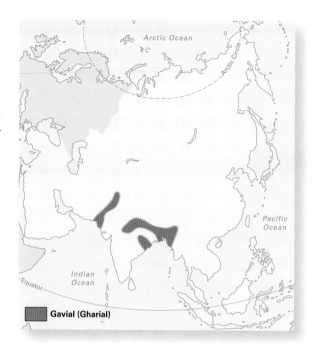
Gavial (Gharial)

Gavials are awkward on land. Unlike other crocodilians, adult gavials are unable to lift their bodies above the ground when on land. Their leg muscles are too weak to support them. They're much more at home in the water.

Habitat. Gavials are known to have once lived in five main river systems—the Indus River in Pakistan; the Ganges River in India and Nepal; the Mahanadi River in India; the Brahmaputra River in Bangladesh, Bhutan, and India; and the Ayeyarwaddy River in Myanmar. Today, these reptiles are found mainly in India and Nepal.

Threats. Gavial populations have long been in decline because of the exploding human population in the region. The decline worsened between the late 1990's and early 2000's. Biologists estimate that gavial numbers fell by roughly 60 percent during that time. The rivers and adjoining land areas inhabited by gavials have been disturbed by people. People have cut down trees and other plant life to obtain firewood and to create cropland and grazing land. They have dug up riverbanks while mining for sand used in construction. Dams have caused some rivers to dry up during part of the year.

Adult male gavials are hunted for the ghara on their snouts and for their genitals, or external sex organs, which are used in folk medicines. Gavial eggs are also collected by people for medicinal purposes. Gavials die when they are accidentally caught in gill nets used by fishermen.

Fishing also reduces the food that gavials need. Gavials are sometimes killed by people who mistakenly believe them to be "man-eaters." In fact, the reptile's snout is too narrow for them to eat anything as large as a person.

Conservation efforts for gavials in India and Nepal—including *captive breeding* (managed breeding) of the animals and their release into protected areas—began during the 1970's. However, their population decline has continued because of disturbances of their *habitat* (living area).

The gavial, unlike other crocodilians, has a long, very narrow snout, which it uses to catch prey.

Varanus komodoensis

Conservation status: Vulnerable

The Komodo dragon is the largest lizard in the world, growing to a length of more than 10 feet (3 meters) and a weight of as much as 365 pounds (165 kilograms). Males are larger than females. Although they don't actually breathe fire like mythological dragons, they do have a somewhat frightening, prehistoric appearance.

Appearance. The body of the Komodo dragon is long and heavy-set with grayish-brown or reddish scales, thick legs with strong claws, and a powerful muscular tail. Their teeth are sharp and sawlike, and their tongues are long, yellow, and forked.

The Komodo dragon kills using a one-two punch of sharp teeth and *venomous* (poisonous) bite. Scientists once thought that the Komodo dragon killed via blood poisoning caused by the multiple strains of bacteria in its saliva.

Komodo dragons often *scavenge* their food (eat dead and decaying animals). Their forked tongues have a special organ of smell that helps them detect rotting flesh from several miles away. They are also good hunters. They run quickly and have the strength to overpower such large mammals as deer, water buffaloes, and wild pigs. Dragons have been known to kill people, including children. These big reptiles take five years to mature after hatching from eggs. They can live for as long as 50 years.

Habitat. The tropical *habitats* (living areas) of Komodo dragons are on the Lesser Sunda Islands of the Indonesian archipelago. These islands include Komodo, Flores, Rinca, and Padar. The animals are usually found on the ground in savanna forests, which are mostly open areas with some tall grasses, bushes, and trees. Dragons may also live in such areas as dried riverbeds, the tops of ridges, and beaches.

Young Komodo dragons, which are much more colorful than adults, are often found in trees.

Threats and conservation. These animals have been protected by law in Indonesia since the 1930's. Nevertheless, the Komodo dragon remains vulnerable to extinction, mainly because its habitat has been degraded and it has been overhunted by people. In addition, *poaching* (illegal hunting) is a big problem. Some dragons are trapped to sell as pets. Others are killed for their body parts, which are used to make traditional remedies. Biologists believe that the wild population of this species today is only a fraction of what it was in the mid-1900's.

There are many Komodo dragons in zoos around the world. These individuals are bred in captivity to help build up the population. More than 18,000 people visit Indonesia's Komodo National Park to see these fascinating reptiles in their natural habitat.

Nipponia nippon

Conservation status: Endangered

The Asian, or Japanese, crested ibis has the long, thin, downward-curving bill that is typical of all ibises. Ibises make up a large group of wading birds found in warm regions throughout the world. This particular *species* (type) has red skin on its face and legs and a crest on its head. The plumage, which is normally bright white, turns gray during the breeding season.

Habitat. The natural *habitat* (living place) of Asian crested ibises consists of *wetlands*, in which they catch fish, frogs, snails, crabs, insects, and other small animals for food. (Wetlands are areas that remain soaked in water for much of the year.) They roost and build their nests in tall trees by the wetlands. They also hunt for food in rice fields and reservoirs near human settlements.

Although the bird's scientific name refers to Japan, the Asian crested ibis is no longer found in the wild in that country. In fact, it is now absent from much of its original, natural *range*, which included Japan, China, Taiwan, the Korean Peninsula, and far eastern Russia. (A range is the area in which an animal normally lives.) The more northern populations in this range used to *migrate* (move) south in autumn, while the more southern populations remained in the same area throughout the year. But the only wild population that exists today is in Shaanxi province in north-central China.

Threats. The Asian ibis remains one of the most endangered *species* (type) of ibis. The birds have become increasingly common in rice fields as their natural wetland habitats have been degraded and reduced in size. People have also converted the birds' wetlands into dry wheat fields, and they have contaminated the wetlands with agricultural chemicals.

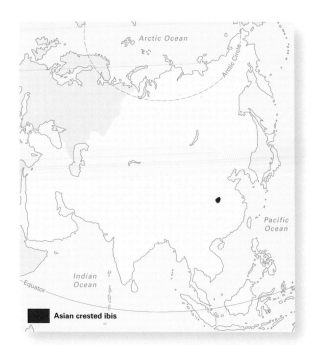

Asian crested ibis

Conservation actions have brought this species back from the brink of extinction. In 1981, there were only seven of the birds known to exist in the wild, all in a mountainous area in China's Shaanxi province. By 2006, biologists estimated that this number had grown to about 500. This limited recovery was made possible by several creative actions involving local people. Volunteers help protect the nests of the ibises by chasing away predators, and they help weak nestlings survive by artificially feeding them. People stock a type of fish called loach in rice paddies to give the ibises food. Education programs help local people better understand the value of preserving the ibis's habitat, of not hunting the birds, and of not using harmful chemical pesticides.

Despite the progress that has been made, the surviving wild population of the Asian crested ibis is still small, and it faces continuing threats.

The Asian crested ibis is no longer found in the wild in Japan. Approximately 500 of the species are known to exist in the wild in China's Shaanxi province.

Polyplectron napoleonis
(P. emphanum)

Conservation status: Vulnerable

The Palawan peacock-pheasant is also known as the Napoleon's peacock-pheasant. Male Palawan peacock-pheasants have long, brightly colored tail feathers in the shape of a fan, similar to the tails of the better-known peacock. The tail has two rows of large, metallic greenish-blue *ocelli* (eye-shaped spots). This same glowing color marks several spots on the male's wings, neck, and head—including a long crest on top of the head. The females lack bright colors and are mostly brownish. Females are also smaller than males. When males and females of the same *species* (type) differ from each other so much, they are said to be "sexually dimorphic."

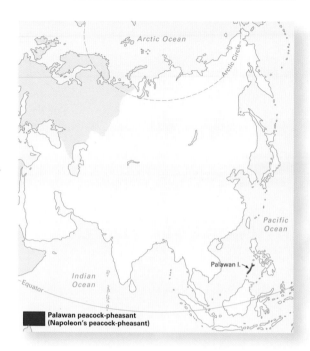

Palawan peacock-pheasant
(Napoleon's peacock-pheasant)

Habitat. Palawan peacock-pheasants feed and nest on the floors of moist forests on the island of Palawan, in the Philippines. They eat a wide variety of foods, including seeds, nuts, fruits, roots, worms, slugs, and insects.

Reproduction. The male shows off his brilliant feathers in courtship dances to attract females. A male begins his dance by spreading his neck feathers and repeatedly bobbing his head up and down. He typically has some kind of food in his beak, such as a piece of fruit, which he drops in front of a female. He next displays his plumage by sticking up the feathers of his head crest and by fanning his raised tail to show all the ocelli. While strutting around performing this display, he also makes a hissing sound.

If the female is impressed with the display, she'll let the male mate with her. Only she—not the male—*incubates* the eggs (keeps them warm so they will hatch). Her drab colors help keep the nest hidden from predators. But the male helps to feed and raise the chicks.

Threats. The destruction of Palawan's forests by logging and mining activities poses a threat to the survival of the peacock-pheasant. Furthermore, these beautiful birds are trapped and hunted for their feathers, which are sold on the international market. The peacock-pheasants themselves are captured live to sell to zoos or bird collectors. Some people kill the birds for food.

Conservation. Most of the activities that threaten Palawan peacock-pheasants are against the law. The birds are legally protected, and their *habitats* (living areas) lie within nature reserves. Nevertheless, the laws are not always enforced. Biologists believe that the population of this species continues to decline.

The brilliant plumage of the Palawan peacock-pheasant is used to attract the female during a courtship dance. The birds have become vulnerable because of that brilliance. Although the Palawan peacock-pheasant is legally protected, the male is hunted for its feathers, which people buy for personal and home decoration.

Gyps bengalensis

Conservation status: Critically Endangered

The white-rumped vulture, also known as the Asian white-backed vulture, has undergone one of the most rapid population crashes known in biology.

Appearance. The white-rumped vulture feeds on *carrion* (dead and decaying animal flesh) and has the naked head that is typical of most birds with that feeding habit. The "white-rumped" name comes from the long white patch of feathers on the bird's otherwise black or gray back.

Habitat. This bird was formerly the most common *species* (type) of vulture in southern and southeastern Asia, as well as one of the most abundant large birds in the world. Its population numbered in the millions. But by the mid-1900's, it had disappeared from most of southeastern Asia. In the 1990's, its numbers began to plummet in India, Pakistan, and elsewhere in the region. Biologists believe that the total global population now numbers only in the thousands.

Threats. What caused this sudden and dramatic decline in the bird's population? The vulture fed on the carcasses of livestock that had been given the drug diclofenac. Farmers widely used this drug to reduce pain in cattle so that the cattle could work longer. The vultures ate the drug with the livestock meat. Diclofenac acted like a poison in the vultures' bodies, preventing their kidneys from functioning, killing the birds.

The poisoning with diclofenac added to other environmental problems that had already put the vulture population on shaky ground. The natural *habitat* (living area) of the vultures— open areas with scattered trees—was replaced by agricultural land, villages, and cities. Although the vultures are adaptable birds that can live near human settlements, the land changes reduced their food and nesting sites. Pesticides and other chemical compounds affected the vultures by sickening or killing them. Still other

White-rumped vulture

pressures on the vulture populations came from the spread of *avian* (bird) malaria and other diseases, from intentional killing by people, and even from strikes by airplanes.

Diclofenac and some of these other problems affecting the white-rumped vulture have harmed other vulture species in the region.

Conservation. Following various government bans on diclofenac in 2000's, some vulture populations began to recover. However, the drug continues to be used illegally by some ranchers, and investigators continue to find the chemical compound in livestock carcasses. A number of white-rumped vultures exist in captivity, serving as a possible source of animals for eventual release into the wild.

Biologists once believed that the white-rumped vulture's naked head and neck were adaptations to help keep the head clean when feeding on carrion. Scientist now believe that the bare skin may play an important role in the regulation of body temperature.

Ailuropoda melanoleuca

Conservation status: Endangered

The giant panda has come to symbolize endangered *species* (types of animals) and the wildlife conservation movement for many people, partly because it is the symbol of the WWF. Formerly known as the World Wildlife Fund, the WWF is one of the world's largest conservation organizations. And the popularity of this animal is not harmed by its resemblance to a cute, oversized, black-and-white teddy bear!

Giant panda

Species. Giant pandas are related to bears, but they differ from other bears in several ways. Their teeth are wide and flat, specialized for chewing bamboo, a tough plant that has poor nutritional value. To get enough nutrition, each panda spends about 14 hours a day eating from 22 to 44 pounds (10 to 20 kilograms) of bamboo. Giant pandas have a modified wrist bone that looks something like a thumb. It helps them grasp bamboo stalks. Adults are huge animals, weighing as much as 300 pounds (136 kilograms). By contrast, newborn pandas are extremely tiny, weighing only about 5 ounces (142 grams).

Habitat and threat. Giant pandas live only in the forests of south-central China. Widespread cutting of these forests for timber and farmland has destroyed much of the *habitat* (living area) of giant pandas. The worst habitat destruction has been in the lowland forests of China.

Conservation. Scientists estimate that fewer than 2,500 giant pandas remain in the wild, mainly in isolated mountain ranges. China's government has tried to protect pandas by establishing reserves of bamboo-rich land. But many of these reserves are separated from each other by farmland and other human *developments* (activities). To help the pandas move from one site to another in their constant search for bamboo, Chinese conservationists have begun to create so-called *wildlife corridors*, strips of protected land that connect larger reserves.

China also has banned logging in many areas and has replanted some forests. However, scientists believe that pandas prefer old-growth forests to replanted forests.

Tough laws against *poaching* (illegal hunting) have been enforced by the Chinese government. Some poachers have even received the death penalty! Less harsh conservation measures include education programs in which villagers are taught the benefits of panda protection.

Other measures to protect giant pandas include breeding them in zoos. Unfortunately, giant pandas do not breed well in captivity. The use of *artificial insemination* (injecting sperm into a female using scientific techniques) has helped pandas reproduce in captivity. There are now about 300 giant pandas in zoos. Scientists plan to eventually introduce some captive-born pandas into the wild.

The giant panda's diet consists of only one staple, bamboo. The Chinese giant panda became endangered when its bamboo forest habitats were cut to create farmland.

Helarctos malayanus

Conservation status: Vulnerable

The Malayan sun bear is the world's smallest bear. It is from 3 to 4 feet (91 to 122 centimeters) long and weighs from 60 to 100 pounds (27 to 45 kilograms).

Appearance. The sun bear's fur color varies greatly, ranging from reddish-brown to gray to black, with a chest patch that may be white, yellow, orange, or speckled. This chest patch is the origin of the sun bear's name. People in ancient times thought that the patch represented the rising sun. Sun bears have a doglike face, giving rise to another name by which they are known—dog bears.

Sun bears have very large paws with no hair on the soles. Their long claws are sharper and more curved than those of other bears.

Habitat and diet. Sun bears use their big feet and sharp claws to climb through trees in their tropical forest *habitat* (living area). They also use them to dig into logs in search of insects to eat. Sun bears eat other foods besides insects. Their diet is *omnivorous,* that is, they will eat just about anything they come across—including fruits, roots, birds, and rodents.

Sun bears are mostly active at night, spending their time lumbering through the trees of lowland forests in Borneo, Indochina, the Malay Peninsula, Myanmar, Sumatra, and Thailand. During the day, they rest in sleeping platforms that they build in the trees out of branches and leaves.

Threats. The massive deforestation that has occurred throughout southeastern Asia since the mid-1900's has drastically reduced the habitat of the Malayan sun bear. Whole forests have been destroyed by the *clearcutting* (total removal) of trees for coffee, rubber, and oil palm plantations; by careless logging practices; and by forest fires. Remaining slices of forest are isolated from each other, making it difficult

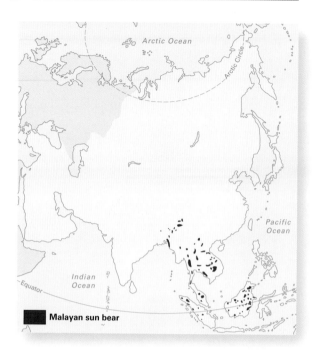

Malayan sun bear

for the sun bears to find enough food to eat and to spread to new areas. Even in forests that still stand, the *ecosystem* (organisms and their physical environment) has been seriously degraded by both human activities and droughts.

Some forests in the region are legally protected as wildlife refuges. But even there, *poachers* (illegal hunters) prey on the sun bears for their body parts and fur, which are sold on the black, or unlawful, market. The gall bladder of captive bears is used to make traditional remedies, and its paws are eaten as delicacies. Adult females are killed so that their cubs can be taken and raised as pets. Farmers kill sun bears because they fear the bears will eat their crops.

Conservation. The Bornean Sun Bear Conservation Centre (BSBCC) in Sepilok, Sabah, Malaysia, rescues captured sun bears. The organization promotes sun bear conservation in Borneo through animal welfare, conservation, rehabilitation, research and education.

The Malayan sun bear, the world's smallest bear, is sometimes called the "dog bear" because of its doglike face.

Nasalis larvatus

Conservation status: Endangered

The proboscis monkey is named for the male's extremely long, bulbous, reddish nose that hangs down over his mouth. The nose gives the monkey a comical appearance. But scientists believe it has a serious purpose. The large nose may make the males' calls louder and more attractive to females.

Appearance. Besides having his distinctive big nose, the male is much larger than the female. Males weigh as much as 52 pounds (24 kilograms), while females weigh no more than 26 pounds (12 kilograms). Proboscis monkeys are born with bright blue faces and silver-blue fur that turns gray after about three months. Adults have reddish hair on their heads, backs, shoulders, and thighs, and pale gray hair on their arms and legs.

Habitat and diet. The natural *habitat*s (living areas) of proboscis monkeys are mangrove forests and lowland rain forests along rivers, swamps, and seacoasts on the island of Borneo in Southeast Asia. Mangrove trees grow in water, with their roots pushing downward from their branches. The roots eventually form a tall network of stilts that hold the tree branches and leaves above the water. Proboscis monkeys spend a lot of time in these trees eating the leaves. They also eat fruits and flowers.

The monkeys have feet with partial webbing between their toes, which makes them good swimmers. However, crocodiles sometimes catch them and eat them when they're swimming.

Threats. Clearing of mangrove trees and other trees along rivers and coasts is the main threat to the proboscis monkey's existence. People cut or burn down the trees to develop agricultural land and oil palm plantations, to harvest timber for construction, and to make room for homes. These activities divide the monkey's natural habitat into small fragments.

Proboscis monkey

Another threat is hunting. Proboscis monkeys are easy to kill in large numbers because they live in groups, and they tend to move slowly. People kill them for food and also to get hard, undigested masses called bezoar stones from the monkeys' intestines. Some people in Asia believe that these bezoar stones are *antidotes* (substances that fight the harmful actions of poisons) or that they possess magical properties. They use the stones to make traditional remedies.

Conservation. Laws in Borneo protect proboscis monkeys from hunting and capture, and several reserves have been established to save this *species* (type of animal). However, *poachers* (illegal hunters) sometimes violate the laws, and the proboscis monkey remains endangered.

Scientists believe the proboscis monkey's long nose may make the males' calls louder and more attractive to females.

Bornean orangutan
Pongo pygmaeus

Conservation status: Endangered

Sumatran orangutan
Pongo abelii

Conservation status: Critically endangered

The name of these red-haired great apes means *person of the forest* in the Malay language. Two *subspecies* (divisions of species) of orangutans live in tropical rain forests on the islands of Borneo and Sumatra in Southeast Asia. Before deforestation destroyed much of their *habitat* (living area), orangutans were found throughout southern China and Southeast Asia.

Appearance. The largest male orangutans stand about 4.5 feet (1.4 meters) tall and weigh about 180 pounds (82 kilograms). Females are much smaller. Mature males typically have wide cheek pads, called flanges, that stick out from the sides of the face.

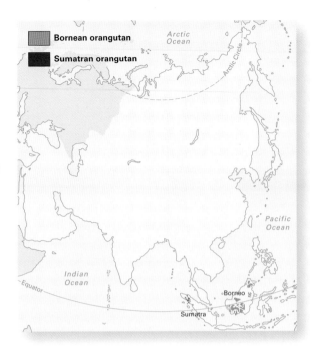

Unlike most apes, the Bornean (below) and Sumatran orangutan actively avoid other members of their kind.

Habitat and diet. Orangutans are the largest mammals that live mostly in trees. They spend more time in trees than any other ape, eating and sleeping high in the treetops and rarely coming to the ground. Their main food is fruit, especially figs. They also eat leaves, bark, insects, and sometimes animal meat.

Reproduction. Compared to chimpanzees and gorillas, orangutans are asocial. That is, they tend to live alone and avoid one another. Males and females come together only to mate. Females produce one infant every seven to nine years, on average.

Threats. The two main threats to orangutans are habitat loss and hunting. Much of the rain forest on Borneo and Sumatra has been converted to plantations for oil palms, as well as acacia, cocoa, rice, and other commercial crops. The oil from oil palms is used for cooking, cosmetics, and industrial applications. Logging activities are another cause of deforestation on these islands. Droughts and fires have further reduced the rain forest habitat.

Sumatran (above) and Bornean orangutans are the largest mammals that live mostly in trees.

As their habitat is cut down, burned, and broken up, orangutan populations become isolated into smaller and smaller groupings. This may result in *inbreeding* (mating of closely related individuals) and a greater risk for disease, increasing the chances for extinction.

Some local people hunt orangutans for their meat, which is sold on the "bushmeat" market, or for other body parts, which are used in traditional medicines. The apes are sometimes killed just to get them out of the way so that people can more easily collect other forest products, such as aloe wood. In addition, females are often killed to collect their infants for sale as pets.

Conservation. Laws designed to protect orangutans from hunting and to preserve their habitat are often ignored. Authorities have rescued many infant orangutans from *poachers* (illegal hunters), raised them in orangutan orphanages, and returned them to the wild.

Panthera uncia

Conservation status: Endangered

The snow leopard is a large cat that lives in the snow-covered mountain ranges of central Asia, including parts of China and Tibet. They make their homes as high as 18,000 feet (5,500 meters) above sea level.

Appearance. The cats have thick, pale gray fur, tinged with tan and sprinkled with black-ish circular spots. Adult snow leopards are from 39 to 51 inches (99 to 130 centimeters) long, not including the tail. Their fluffy tail adds an extra 3.3 feet (1 meter). The cats use it to help maintain their balance on steep, rocky slopes.

Diet. Snow leopards are powerful, athletic hunters capable of killing prey as much as three times their own weight. They eat main-ly wild sheep and goats, but also birds, small mammals, and livestock. They hunt like a giant house cat, quietly and expertly stalking their prey before suddenly pouncing on it. Snow leopards are great jumpers. They have been seen to leap as far as 50 feet (15 meters).

Threats. Biologists estimate that fewer than 7,000 snow leopards remain in the wild. Their population has declined mainly because of loss of their *habitat* (living areas), reduced numbers of the animals they prey on, and *poaching* (illegal hunting).

Much of the snow leopard's habitat has been converted into agricultural land. The natural prey of snow leopards became hard to find after local farmers and ranchers moved their livestock onto the high-altitude grass-lands where the cats live. Competition with the livestock means that the wild prey have less plant food on which to graze. Moreover, people hunt some of the snow leopard's prey. As a result of the loss of their natural food animals, some snow leopards resort to killing livestock. Herders then kill the leopards in response.

Snow leopard

Snow leopards are also killed illegally for their pelts, which are used to make luxurious coats, and their bones and internal organs, which are used to make traditional medicines. A full-length snow leopard coat may sell for as much as $60,000 on the black, or unlawful, market. Snow leopard pelts are viewed as a type of trophy by some poachers.

Conservation. Some of the snow leopard's habitat is protected by law. But these big cats are wide-ranging animals, and many protected areas are too small to be effective refuges.

Approximately 500 snow leopards live in zoos around the world. Some of these zoos are part of an international program to breed the cats in captivity to build up the population for eventual release into the wild.

Under the direction of various zoos, the snow leopard is being bred in captivity to increase its population. Eventually, these "city cats" will be released into the wild.

Panthera tigris

Conservation status: Endangered

The tiger is the largest member of the cat family. Males are about 9 feet (2.7 meters) long, including a 3-foot (0.9-meter) tail, and weigh about 420 pounds (190 kilograms). Females are shorter and less heavy. Tigers are famous for their bold black stripes on a coat that ranges in color from brownish-yellow to orange-red. The stripe pattern of each tiger is as unique as a person's fingerprint.

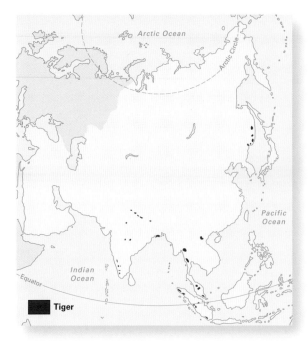

Habitat and diet. Most tigers live in parts of southern Asia, especially in India and Thailand. A few live in eastern Siberia. Tigers once had a much wider *range* throughout southern Asia. (A range is the area in which a species lives naturally.) In the 1800's, however, people started killing tigers in large numbers and clearing the forests in which they lived.

Scientists identify eight *subspecies* (divisions of species) of tigers: the Bali, Bengal, Caspian, Javan, Northern Indochinese, Siberian (or Amur), South China, and Sumatran tigers. The Bali, Caspian, and Javan subspecies are thought to be extinct. All remaining subspecies are endangered. The most endangered are believed to be the Siberian, South China, and Sumatran tigers.

Tigers prey on the largest animals found in their territories, including antelope, deer, wild cattle, wild pigs—and even young rhinoceroses and elephants. They also catch such smaller animals as monkeys, peafowl, and frogs.

Threats. The main reasons that tigers are endangered are hunting, loss of *habitat* (living area), and loss of prey. Killing of tigers for trophies was very common in the 1800's and early 1900's. South China tigers were frequently killed as pests in China until the late 1970's, when the government made it illegal to kill them. It is illegal to kill any wild tigers today. However, the cats are still killed by livestock owners, who view them as threats to their

animals, and by *poachers* (illegal hunters), who kill them for their bones and other body parts. The body parts are sold on the black, or unlawful, market for use in traditional Chinese remedies.

The loss of the tiger's habitat is the result of Asia's exploding human population, which has expanded into formerly natural areas. In addition, the tiger's natural prey has been reduced by human hunters, causing tigers in some areas to kill domestic cattle and water buffalo. This leads, in turn, to more killing of tigers as pests.

Conservation. Tigers are protected inside nature reserves and national parks in some countries, including India and Nepal. There are also many tigers in zoos, especially Bengal and Siberian tigers. Unlike some endangered animals, tigers breed well in captivity.

Economic development and population density on the island of Sumatra have eroded the rain forest habitat of the Sumatran tiger. The subspecies on nearby Java is thought to be extinct.

Platanista gangetica

Conservation status: Endangered

The Ganges River dolphin is a nearly blind *cetacean* that lives in the dark, muddy waters of rivers in northern India and Pakistan. (Cetacean is the scientific name for dolphins and whales.) Some scientists classify it as the same *species* (type) as the Indus River dolphin. Other scientists recognize the Indus River dolphin as a separate species, named *P. minor.*

Appearance and navigation. All river dolphins differ from their more famous marine cousins by having smaller eyes and a longer *snout* (beak). Because their vision is so poor, these animals rely on *echolocation* to navigate and find their food. In echolocation, a dolphin makes a series of clicking sounds and listens for the echoes that reflect back from objects. The echoes tell the dolphin the location of the objects.

Ganges River dolphin

Threats. The aquatic *habitat* (living area) of the Ganges River dolphin changed for the worse as the human population in the region exploded in the last century. *Toxic* (poisonous) chemical compounds from agricultural and industrial *developments* (human activities) polluted the dolphins' river systems. Sand mining (for construction) also harmed the natural river *ecosystems.* (An ecosystem is made up of living animals and their physical environment.)

These rivers were further modified by more than 50 dams, which changed the water flow and water levels in the rivers and isolated small populations of the dolphins from one another. This isolation means that dolphins cannot travel as widely as they once did to meet dolphins in other areas. As a result, scientists fear that dolphins in many areas may resort to *inbreeding.* Such mating with related individuals makes populations weaker and less able to survive diseases, pollution, and other challenges.

Canals are another river development that has caused problems. Some dolphins that swim into human-made canals are unable to find their way back to their river habitats.

Some people in India and Pakistan hunt river dolphins as a source of meat or oil (which is used as fish bait). Fishermen sometimes accidentally kill the dolphins when the animals get caught and drown in fishing nets.

Conservation. The Ganges River dolphin is now legally protected in much of its remaining *range* (area in which it lives naturally). India and Pakistan have established a number of national parks and wildlife sanctuaries in which the dolphins live. Laws against *poaching* (illegal hunting) are being increasingly enforced. A special conservation program rescues dolphins trapped in fishing nets. Although progress has been made to protect the Ganges River dolphin, many conservationists believe that more action is needed to ensure the survival of the species.

The Ganges River dolphin has very poor eyesight and uses echolocation to navigate. The dolphin makes a series of clicking sounds and listens for the echoes to reflect back from objects.

Elephas maximus

Conservation status: Endangered

Elephants are the largest animals that live on land today, though the Asian elephant is smaller than its African relative. An Asian bull can grow to a shoulder height of about 10.5 feet (3.2 meters) and a weight of 8,000 pounds (3,600 kilograms). African bulls, by contrast, can stand 11 feet (3.4 meters) high and weigh 12,000 pounds (5,400 kilograms). The ears of Asian elephants are only about half as large as those of African elephants. Also, Asian elephants' tusks are shorter.

Habitat. Asian elephants live in forests in India and Southeast Asia. These animals used to have a wider *range* (area in which they lived naturally), but they are now extinct in western Asia and most of China.

Threats. Human land *developments* (activities) are causing the Asian elephant's forest *habitat* (living area) to shrink, and *poachers* (illegal hunters) kill the males for their ivory tusks. The threats faced by African elephants are similar, though less serious. African elephants' numbers have rebounded as a result of many years of conservation activities. Biologists estimate that the wild Asian population—perhaps about 50,000—is only one-tenth the size of the wild African population. Roughly 15,000 Asian elephants exist in captivity. Unlike the African elephant, the Asian elephant can be trained. They have long been used as work animals.

Human population growth in southern and southeastern Asia has led to the loss of much of the region's forested area as people created farmland, roads, villages, and cities. The forests were also cut down to obtain timber for construction. As a result, the elephants' natural habitat was carved into smaller and smaller fragments. The plants in these fragments cannot support as many elephants as the vegetation in the original, larger forest.

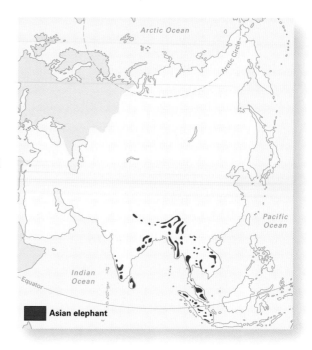

Asian elephant

As they search for more plants to eat and other elephants to meet, some Asian elephants wander onto farmland. Farmers often kill these elephants to protect their crops and property.

The poaching of bull Asian elephants for their ivory tusks has affected elephant populations in two ways. It has reduced the total number of elephants, and it has caused some wild populations to have far fewer males than females. Together, both results greatly endanger the survival of the species.

Conservation. Many Asian nations have set aside national parks and other reserves to protect elephant habitats. But this land may not be big enough to fully protect such a large mammal, which requires a great deal of food and a wide range in which to roam.

The Asian elephant is endangered mainly due to loss of habitat and hunting. Although the trade in ivory is illegal in many countries, poachers still kill elephants and sell the ivory on the black, or unlawful, market.

Rhinoceros sondaicus

Conservation status: Critically endangered

The Javan rhinoceros is one of three *species* (types) of rhinoceros that live in Asia. It once ranged from eastern Bengal into Myanmar, and southward to Java, Borneo, and Sumatra.

Appearance and habitat. The Javan rhinoceros stands about 5.5 feet (1.7 meters) tall and weighs from 1 ton to 2.5 tons (0.9 metric ton to 2.3 metric tons). It has only one horn. It is found most often near water in tropical rain forests.

Threats. The Javan rhinoceros is now nearly extinct. Fewer than 50 adults may exist in the wild, all in a single national park in Java. In 2012, the animal was added to the IUCN's list of the 100 most endangered species. In fact, it may be the rarest large mammal in the world.

There are several reasons for its rarity. Many rhinos disappeared from Vietnam as a result of the war that raged in that nation during the 1960's and 1970's. Land mines, chemical herbicides, destruction of *habitat* (living area), and other problems related to the war took their toll on the species. The rhino was declared extinct in Vietnam in 2010.

Elsewhere in the region, the main threats to the Javan rhino's survival have been loss of habitat to farmland and human settlements, and *poaching* (illegal hunting) for its horn and other body parts, which are used in traditional Chinese medicines. *Inbreeding* (mating between related individuals) in the rhino's tiny remaining populations weakens the species.

Conservation. The breeding population of Javan rhinos exists in the Ujung Kulon National Park. The International Rhino Foundation (IRF)-funded Rhino Protection Units have kept the Ujung Kulon population safe from poaching.

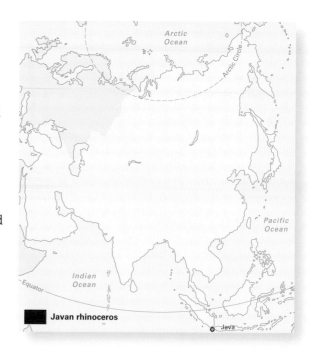

Javan rhinoceros

The Javan rhinoceros lives near rivers and other bodies of water in tropical rain forests.

Dicerorhinus sumatrensis

Conservation status: Critically endangered

Like the Javan rhinoceros, the Sumatran rhino is nearly extinct.

Appearance. Unlike the one-horned Javan and Indian rhinos, the Sumatran rhinoceros has two horns. It is about 4.5 feet (1.4 meters) tall and weighs about 1 ton (0.9 metric ton). It has more hair, especially on its tail and ears, than the other Asian rhinos.

Habitat. The Sumatran rhino, compared with the more abundant cousin, the Indian rhinoceros, is a relatively small rhino that is native to Borneo, Sumatra, and the Malay Peninsula.

Threats. The two major threats to the survival of the Sumatran rhino are habitat destruction for timber and farmland and poaching for the animal's horns and other body parts, which are used in traditional remedies. The remaining population of Sumatran rhinos is now so small and fragmented that low birth rates and inbreeding could prevent it from ever fully recovering.

Conservation. The population of this species was in a rapid free fall until the 1990's, when better protection slowed the decline. Still, the total population today may be fewer than 275 individuals.

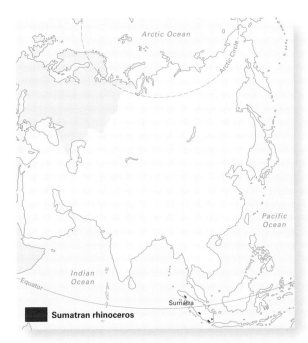

Unlike the Indian and Javan rhinos, the Sumatran rhinoceros has two horns and more hair.

Equus ferus przewalskii

Conservation status: Endangered

The Przewalski's horse is a *subspecies* of wild horse that is the only true wild horse in existence today. (A subspecies is a variation of a *species* [type of animal].) Other types of horses thought of as wild, such as the mustangs in the western United States, are descendants of runaway domestic horses.

The tongue-twisting name of this horse comes from the Russian explorer Nikolai M. Przewalski *(puhr zheh VAHL skihz),* who first described the subspecies scientifically in the 1870's. However, people have long known about these wild horses. Some cave paintings in Europe that were made more than 20,000 years ago seem to show Przewalski's horses.

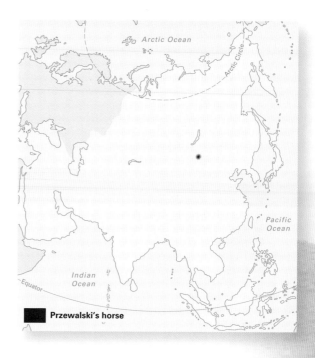

Przewalski's horse

Appearance. The Przewalski's horse has a stocky, donkeylike body with short legs, a short neck, and a strong jaw. It stands about 53 inches (135 centimeters) tall at the shoulder.

Habitat. The horse grazes on vegetation on *steppes* (dry plains covered with short grasses) and shrubland. Until the late 1700's, Przewalski's horse ranged from Germany and Russia eastward to Mongolia and northern China. Its population then began a drastic decline.

Threats. The decline of the Przewalski's horse resulted from excessive hunting by people, as well as by the loss of grazing land to cattle and other domestic livestock. Another problem was *crossbreeding* (mixing types) with domesticated horses. The resulting hybrid offspring lacked the special physical traits of Przewalski's horses. Still another challenge was the spread of disease. Adding to these problems was the fact that Przewalski's horses have a slow rate of reproduction. The mare gives birth to a single foal after a year-long pregnancy.

By the 1960's, the Przewalski's horse was considered to be extinct in the wild, though many of the animals lived in zoos and other sanctuaries.

Conservation. Since the 1990's, hundreds of captive-bred Przewalski's horses have been released into the wild, in the steppes of Mongolia. These releases have been part of an effort to reestablish the horses in their natural *habitat* (living area).

Although not all of the released animals have survived, scientists think the wild population is increasing. Still, the number of the horses remains small, and biologists must carefully monitor the animals to make sure they are doing well. Drought, disease, and other problems can pose serious challenges for the wild population. But despite ongoing problems, the Przewalski's horse represents a success story for conservation.

The Przewalski's horse is the world's only true wild horse. Its habitat are steppes—dry plains covered in short grasses. Conservationists have released captive-bred Przewalski's horses on the steppes of Mongolia.

Glossary

Antidote Substances that fight the harmful actions of poisons.

Artificial insemination The introduction of a male's sperm into a female's body using scientific techniques.

Avian Having to do with birds.

Captive breeding The breeding of a species in a nonnatural place to build up the population.

Carapace The shell or other hard covering on the back or top of an animal.

Carrion Dead and decaying animal flesh.

Cetacean Scientific name for dolphins and whales.

Clearcutting Cutting down all the trees in an area of forest.

Crossbreeding Producing offspring by mating of two different species.

Deciduous A tree that loses its leaves at a certain time each year and later grows new leaves.

Development Refers to farmland, cities, dams, roads, or other changes that destroy the natural environment.

Echolocation A system in which certain animals make sounds and listen for the echoes, helping the animals navigate.

Ecosystem A natural system made up of living organisms and their physical environment.

Habitat The type of environment in which an organism lives.

Inbreeding Breeding of closely related individuals, often leading to the weakening of a species.

Incubation Keeping eggs warm, usually by sitting on them, so that they will hatch.

Invertebrate An animal without a backbone.

Migrate To travel from one region to another, often with a change in the seasons.

Nocturnal Active at night.

Ocelli Eye-shaped spots.

Omnivorous Eating a wide variety of both animal and vegetable food.

Osteoderms Hard, bony plates.

Poaching The illegal killing of an animal.

Pores Holes in the skin.

Prehensile Able to grasp and hold on to something.

Range The area in which certain plants or animals live or naturally occur.

Scavenge Feed on dead and decaying matter.

Silt Tiny pieces of sand, clay, or other matter carried by moving water

Snout The front of an animal's head, containing the nose, mouth, and jaws.

Spawn Lay eggs.

Species A group of animals or plants that have certain permanent characteristics in common and are able to interbreed.

Steppes Dry plains covered in short grasses.

Subspecies A group of organisms that are more closely related to each other than to other members of the same species.

Toxic Poisonous.

Venomous Poisonous.

Wetland Land where the ground remains soaked with water for most of the year.

Wildlife corridor A strip of protected land that connects larger reserves, allowing animals to travel between the reserves.

Books

Animal Encyclopedia: 2,500 Animals with Photos, Maps, and More! Washington, DC: National Geographic, 2012. Print.

Hammond, Paula. *The Atlas of Endangered Animals: Wildlife Under Threat Around the World.* Tarrytown, NY: Marshall Cavendish, 2010. Print.

Hoare, Ben, and Tom Jackson. *Endangered Animals.* New York: DK Pub., 2010. Print.

Silhol, Sandrine, Gaëlle Guérive, and Marie Doucedame. *Extraordinary Endangered Animals.* New York: Abrams Books for Young Readers, 2011. Print.

Weston, Christopher, and Art Wolfe. *Animals on the Edge: Reporting from the Frontline of Extinction.* New York: Thames & Hudson, 2009. Print.

Websites

Arkive. Wildscreen, 2014. Web. 14 May 2014.

"Asia." *Zoological Society of London.* Zoological Society of London, n.d. Web. 21 May 2014.

"Asian Wildlife." *BBC Nature.* BBC, 2014. Web. 21 May 2014.

"Endangered Species." *BBC Bitesize Science.* BBC, 2014. Web. 21 May 2014.

"Especies Fact Sheets." *Kids' Planet.* Defenders of Wildlife, n.d. Web. 14 May 2014.

Tregaskis, Shiona. "The world's extinct and endangered species – interactive map." *The Guardian.* Guardian News and Media Limited, 3 Sept. 2012. Web. 14 May 2014.

Organizations *for helping endangered animals*

Wildlife Conservation Society – Asian Elephant
The Wildlife Conservation Society, founded in 1895, has the clear mission to save wildlife and wild places across the globe.
http://www.wcs.org/saving-wildlife/elephants/asian-elephant.aspx

Defenders of Wildlife
Founded in 1947, Defenders of Wildlife is a major national conservation organization focused on wildlife and habitat conservation.
http://www.defenders.org/take-action

National Geographic – Big Cats Initiative
National Geographic, along with Dereck and Beverly Joubert, launched the Big Cats Initiative to raise awareness and implement change to the dire situation facing big cats.
http://animals.nationalgeographic.com/animals/big-cats-initiative/

National Geographic – The Ocean Initiative
National Geographic's Ocean Initiative helps identify and support individuals and organizations that are using creative and entrepreneurial approaches to marine conservation.
http://ocean.nationalgeographic.com/ocean/about-ocean-initiative

National Wildlife Federation – Adoption Center
Symbolically adopt your favorite species and at the same time support the National Wildlife Federation's important work protecting wildlife and connecting people to nature.
http://www.shopnwf.org/Adoption-Center/index.cat

Neighbor Ape
Neighbor Ape strives to conserve the habitat of wild chimpanzees in southeastern Senegal, to protect the chimpanzees themselves, and to provide for the well-being of the Senegalese people who have traditionally lived in the area alongside these chimpanzees.
http://www.globalgiving.org/donate/10235/neighbor-ape/

Smithsonian National Zoo – Adopt a Species
The Adopt a Species program supports the National Zoo's extraordinary work in the conservation and care of the world's rarest animals.
http://nationalzoo.si.edu/support/adoptspecies/

World Wildlife Fund
World Wildlife Fund works in 100 countries and is supported by over 1 million members in the United States and close to 5 million globally.
http://www.worldwildlife.org/how-to-help

Index

Acknowledgments

The publishers acknowledge the following sources for illustrations. Credits read from top to bottom, left to right, on their respective pages. All maps, charts, and diagrams were prepared by the staff unless otherwise noted.

COVER © Holger Ehlers, Alamy Images;
© Jamie Marshall, Alamy Images
4   © Jamie Marshall, Alamy Images
6   © Michael D. Kern, Nature Picture Library
7   © WILDLIFE/Alamy Images
8   © Juniors Bildarchiv/Alamy Images
9   © Wasan Gredpree, Colourbox
10 © Ryu Uchiyama, Nature Production/ Minden Pictures
13 © FLPA/Alamy Images
15 © Melvyn Longhurst, SuperStock
17 © Dr. Axel Gebauer, Nature Picture Library
18 © Michael Pitts, Nature Picture Library
21 © Xi Zhinong, Nature Picture Library

23 © Marc Anderson, Alamy Images
25 © FLPA/Alamy Images
27 © Thinkstock
29 © Gerry Ellis, Minden Pictures
31 © Fiona Rogers, Nature Picture library
32 © blickwinkel/Alamy Images
33 © Cultura RM/Alamy Images
35 © Dietmar Nill, Nature Picture Library
37 © tbk Media/Alamy Images
39 © Roland Seitre, Nature Picture Library
41 © Justine Pickett, Papilio/Alamy Images
42 © Mary Plage, Oxford Scientific/Getty Images
43 © David Tipling, Nature Picture Library
45 © Heather Angel, Natural Visions/Alamy Images

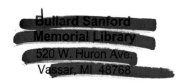
DATE DUE

PRINTED IN U.S.A.